Summary and ~~~~

The President

ᵇy

Bill Clinton and James Patterson

Nosco Publishing

Note to readers:
This is an unofficial summary and analysis of Bill Clinton and James Pattersons's *The President is Missing: A Novel* designed to enrich your reading experience.

Attention: Our Gift to You

As a way of thanking you for purchasing *this* book, we would like to give you another book as a gift: *Stoicism: The Art of Living a Modern Stoic and Happy Life Now.*

If you would like a copy, please visit:
http://NoscoPublishing.com/offer/
Regards,
Nosco Publishing

Table of Contents

BOOK SUMMARY

Former President Bill Clinton and bestselling novelist James Patterson constructed a spellbinding thriller; *The President is Missing,* which showcased the vulnerability of the United States to terrorist activities in cyberspace. This fast-moving tale centered on Jon Duncan, a fictional commander in chief who brimmed with courage, humanity, and stoicism. Duncan, the protagonist, faced the confluence of interrelated threats that included cyber terror, espionage, a life-threatening health condition, and a traitor in the cabinet.

Contrary to the title, the president was never really missing. Duncan assessed the high-stakes threat and determined that he could only deal with the enemy was by going underground, away from the eyes of his political and international foes. The novel began with a mock trial staged to prepare Duncan for a congressional inquiry investigating his botched attempts to capture a foreign terrorist. During the mock trial, Duncan lost his composure and showed his temper. His advisers cautioned him not to appear before an actual committee because of his emotional fervor. Throughout the book, the congressional hearing and the threat of impeachment loomed.

When a young female terrorist approached Duncan's daughter, Lilly, in Paris and uttered the code words *Dark Ages,* the president's attention was riveted. Trial terror attacks followed, making Duncan realize that the young woman was a legitimate threat. The cyber terrorists even managed to infiltrate the seemingly impenetrable White House system, causing lights to flicker off and on randomly. Duncan met privately with the young woman, Nina, only to end the meeting with more questions than answers.

Nina sent Duncan to a baseball game with her young partner, a genius hacker named Augie to learn more about the cyber threat. Duncan had to attend the meeting without his typical convey of Secret Service protectors, putting himself in imminent danger. Duncan was a grieving widower and a devoted single father. His last act before breaking free from the Secret Service was to stare at a photograph of his late wife and feel the flood of emotions that he experienced during her bout with cancer. After declaring his undying love, Duncan entered the subterranean tunnels under the White House and drove to the apartment of an old female friend. She helped him create a disguise, which he wore to meet Augie at a baseball stadium. Duncan's willingness to meet unvetted informants without security showed the protagonist's reckless abandon. When assassins nearly gunned Duncan and Augie down after the meeting, Duncan gave the young terrorist instant credibility.

The writers created geopolitical intrigue including Russian interference, threats against the Saudi King, and the cyberattack directed by the Sons of Jihad, a bloodthirsty terrorist organization. Jon Duncan summoned leaders from Israel, Germany, and Russia on a high-stakes summit designed to save developed nations from impending destruction.

The main story line followed a sometimes-rogue president who was battling a potentially fatal blood disorder while he struggled to identify the traitor in his inner circle. Additionally, assassins targeted Duncan and Augie, including a stunning female marksman with a one hundred percent kill rate.

The following chapters recounted the Duncan's race against the clock to stop the cyber-attack. Throughout the book, the writers provided well-crafted plot twists. They created a national awareness of the very real vulnerability of the United States against a few tech-savvy people intent on mass destruction.

SETTING FOR THE STORY

The setting for this story included the White House and a remote cabin in Virginia. Both locations had highly protected areas where Secret Service controlled access. At the site in Virginia, the rural outdoor area provided secluded places for meetings but also afforded opportunities for the terrorists to hide. Even with careful Secret Service vigilance, neither location was impenetrable.

STORY PLOT ANALYSIS

The story was a classic tale of good and evil presented in a fast-moving plot involving the destruction of the United States at the hands of young, tech-savvy terrorists. Because one of the writers was Bill Clinton, the reader had access to a rare vantage point regarding White House operations. Two computer geeks collaborated with one of the world's most brutal terrorists to produce a seemingly unstoppable computer virus with the potential to destroy modern civilization. The devastation potential was so huge that Duncan called it *Dark Ages*.

There were two sub-plots woven into the main story line. President Jon Duncan, a widower with a daughter, was trying to face down the computer virus while dealing with a blood disorder, which had the potential to cause a stroke or internal bleed. He did not want to leave his daughter as an orphan, but he put his own life on the line to protect the nation.

Additionally, Duncan had to look at his most trusted advisors and try to find out which one betrayed him and the country. The obvious candidate was his vice president. He was ultimately saddened to find out that his trusted chief of staff was the traitor.

Both writers skillfully wove the three plots together to create a suspenseful page-turner.

MAIN AND SECONDARY CHARACTER LIST

Main Characters

Jon Duncan: The hero of the book, Duncan was the rouge president who handled his office with courage and an unwavering independence. He was equal parts brave and brilliant; his ability to make quick decisions saved the nation from certain destruction.

Augie: He was in his early twenties and worked with his paramour, Nina. He was slim, like her with an eastern European bone structure. Augie tried to let Duncan know that a computer virus was imminent in the United States. Augie tried to dismantle the virus but his knowledge about the design of the computer virus was limited because his specialty was hacking.

Nina: Nina was the edgy computer genius who went to Lilly initially and mentioned *Dark Ages*. The waif thin Eastern European wore jeans and had half of her head shaved when she entered the White House to meet with Duncan to warn him about the threat to America's computer systems. Nina was once Suliman's love interest, but she left him for Augie.

Suliman Cindoruk: Suliman, leader of the Sons of Jihad, was wealthy and powerful. He worked with Augie, Nina, and other experts to develop a terrorist network capable of destroying the computer systems in the United States, plunging the nation into the *Dark Ages*. He was decadent morally and cared only about his personal interests.

Bach: She was the stunning Russian assassin who had killed on every continent. Using her semi-automatic rifle, she beheaded a prosecutor in Colombia and killed the leader of a rebel army in Darfur. She had an astounding 100% kill rate when she arrived in Washington to assassinate her target. Bach was a complicated woman who killed to get the resources she needed to create a life of safety and love for her unborn child.

Carolyn Brock: She was friend and highly trusted Chief of Staff for President Duncan. She was a former congressional representative who was on her way to become Speaker of the House when a derogatory comment she made accidentally on a live mike became public. She was the person who betrayed the president.

Kathy Brandt: She was the Vice President under President Duncan. She was a prime suspect as the traitor in the inner circle. Although she conspired with Lester Rhodes to oust Duncan, Brant did not betray her country to the terrorists.

Secondary Characters

Lester Rhodes: He was the Speaker of the House who ardently wanted to use his power to remove President Duncan from office. He accused President Duncan of being disloyal to the United States and instead giving support to the Sons of Jihad, a terrorist organization. Rhodes had his own agenda; he offered to help the vice president replace Duncan if the vice president would appoint Rhodes's daughter to the Supreme Court.

Sons of Jihad: This was a terrorist group determined to destroy the United States. The group had access to the most technologically skillful computer experts on earth.

Rachael Duncan: Although Rachael was dead, she was a prominent character throughout the story. Rachael was the president's late wife who died at an early age from cancer. She was brilliant and beautiful, and he remained devoted to her memory.

Deborah Lane: She was a hematologist who worked at Georgetown Hospital. Although she was not President Duncan's regular doctor, she treated him for his life-threatening blood disorder. She stressed that he could die from a stroke or internal bleed, but he refused treatment that might compromise his cognitive abilities. They compromised on treatment that kept him alive but preserved his capacity to function in office. She was a strong, knowledgeable character. Lane consistently stood up to President Duncan and was firm in her recommendations.

Danny Akers: He was the White House counsel who grew up as a next-door neighbor to President Duncan. They shared many experiences together and their loyalty was important to Duncan. Akers was a scholar who left his law firm to work in the US Court of Appeals before his came to the White House.

JoAnn: She was Duncan's trusted secretary.

Alex Trimble: With a barrel chest and buzz cut, Alex looked like a Secret Service man. He oversaw Duncan's security detail and he ran the operation as efficiently as a military operation.

Brendan Mohan: He was the National Security Advisor.

Erica Beatty: Beatty was the CIA Director, a bookish soft-spoken woman with eyes like a racoon and cropped gray hair. She spent her entire career in the CIA.

Mandy: She was a famous, beautiful actress who was friends with Duncan and his late wife. She helped him to put on make-up and disguises that allowed him to go out without being easily recognized.

Ranko: Bach's mentor was a Serbian soldier who took pity on her after Serbian troops killed her father. He taught her to shoot and became her lover.

Elizabeth Greenfield: She was the newly minted FBI Director confronted with the *Dark Ages* threat approximately six weeks after taking office.

Greg Morton: He was Carolyn Brock's husband who welcomed Duncan and his team in a secluded, safe location away from the terrorists.

Noya Baram: The Israeli leader who came to the Summit to discuss the computer virus threat.

President Chernokey: He was the leader of Russia.

Chancellor Richter: He was the German leader who came to the summit.

Devin and Casey: They were two computer experts who attempted to use their knowledge to stop the computer virus.

ANALYSIS OF KEY CHARACTERS

Carolyn Brock: She was the trusted White House Chief of Staff for President Duncan. Before coming to the White House, Brock was a three-term progressive who managed to win a conservative House district in Ohio. She moved quickly up the ranks of the House leadership and was on track to become the Speaker of the House. Brock was telegenic, intelligent, and personable. Fundraisers loved her, and she achieved the pinnacle of House leadership by age forty. Her meteoric rise to the top derailed when one of her political opponents made a derogatory comment about her husband, a noted trial lawyer. Brock called the opponent an obscene name in front of a live mike, a comment picked up by the Internet and cable news. She admitted to the comment and noted that if a man had said the same words, it would not have been an issue. Her conservative base did not approve of her profane comments and she lost her next election. Throughout the book, Brock was professional and calm in dealing with the impending crisis facing the nation. She had the perfect veneer of commitment to President Duncan. Brock skillfully shifted suspicion for her betrayal to the vice-president. She conclusively revealed her involvement accidentally when President Duncan convened his inner circle to try to crack the password needed to stop a total national collapse of the Internet. Brock did not intentionally mean to get involved with the plot, but she did not reveal information in a timely manner to her boss and the intelligence community. That misstep put the nation at risk. Ultimately, she cracked under pressure and revealed her deep resentment regarding Duncan.

Jon Duncan- As the president, Jon was the protagonist and hero of the book. His father, a high-school math teacher, died in a car crash when he was four and his mother supported him by waiting tables at Curly Ray's restaurant. Duncan played pro-ball in Double A and he was a hero as a Ranger in Desert Storm. His beloved wife passed away from cancer and he frequently remembered his devotion to her. Duncan was a single father who cared deeply about his daughter and did everything he could to keep her safe. He was a brilliant politician who understood the challenges associated with potential political enemies. As the protagonist, Duncan was willing to risk his political career and face impeachment rather than put America in peril by revealing secret information about the people who threatened to dismantle the Internet, leaving the nation vulnerable to attack and certain destruction. He was skillful in dealing with political enemies, but he also knew that many of the politicians were more interested in their careers than in protecting the country. Duncan had a life-threatening blood disorder that often made him weak and dizzy. Without treatment, he was vulnerable to a stroke or internal hemorrhage, which could be fatal. Duncan carefully balanced the risks to keep himself both healthy enough to function and alert enough to make sound decisions. He did not want to make his daughter an orphan, but he knew that the future of the nation depended on him. Duncan struggled with physical problems associated with his blood disorder, which made it challenging for him to function effectively. He also had to deal with his inner circle of trusted advisors while he tried to determine which one betrayed the nation to the terrorists. Throughout much of the book, he was at risk physically from both the terrorists and from his own blood disorder.

Bach-She was the beautiful, pregnant Russian assassin. Her life was a contradiction; she thought it was cruel to eat meat, but she willingly killed humans. She loved classical music, historical attractions, and culture while she lived a life of brutality and death. She selected her favorite composer's name as her pseudonym. She thought about her mother and brother and remembered their early years together. Her brother was a married musician with two children. In many ways, she was reaching for the same kind of normal life filled with love. When her assignment ended, she expected to have enough money to raise her own child in safety and security. To achieve this goal, she had to do unspeakable things including using her body sexually and as a weapon to achieve her objectives. Serbian soldiers killed her father and sexually attacked her when she hunted for rice, bread, or firewood. She retaliated, and her mother was killed, causing her brother to blame her. One of the Serbian insurgents, Ranko, took pity on her and gave her lessons on shooting with accuracy. He also became her lover.

Nina: She was a young, complicated computer genius. At an early age, she encountered political violence that badly injured her. Later, she met Suliman and became romantically involved. Using her extraordinary knowledge about technology, Nina created a virus with the capability to wipe out computers immediately. This dangerous computer virus had the potential to shut down every computer in the United States, making the entire national vulnerable. She later left Suliman and became involved with Augie. Nina eventually did not want to destroy the United States so she and Augie devised a plan to inform Duncan that Suliman had access to a computer virus, which could bring about the dreaded *Dark Ages*. Suliman's team assassinated her shortly after Duncan met with Augie. Even the most technologically advanced members of the President's team could not dismantle the perfectly crafted virus.

Augie: A young computer hacker, Augie was a genius at technology. He initially became involved with the terrorist group, but he did not want to be involved with mass destruction, so he worked with Nina to warn Duncan and save America. Augie was genuinely in love with Nina and he respected her brilliance. He was full of false bravado, but he also was afraid of the circumstances that spun totally out of control. Augie was in over his head and he was not at all certain how to correct the problems that he and Nina helped to create.

Katherine: She made no secret of the fact that she wanted to be president, not vice president and she was willing to compromise her principals to get to the Oval Office. Although she was a flawed character, she was not the villain although throughout much of the book she seemed to be the likely culprit.

Lester Rhodes: He was an ambitious, slimy politician who was willing to use his influence to put Katherine in the Oval Office in exchange for his daughter's appointment to the Supreme Court. Lester was transparent in his vile ambition to advance his personal interests.

Suliman Cindoruk: He was a ruthless killer and the leader of a terrorist organization. His interests were centered around his desire for power and wealth and he had no regard for the people he hurt. He was willing to destroy the United States and kill countless people to advance his own mission. Ironically, he was a coward, unable to take his own life when he was captured.

Enjoying this book so far?

We would like to ask you for a favor: would you be kind enough to leave a quick review for this book on Amazon? It would be greatly appreciated!

CHAPTER SUMMARIES

Chapter One: The House Select Committee, under the direction of Lester Rhodes, Speaker of the House, convened to interrogate President Duncan. They accused him of protecting terrorists, specifically the Sons of Jihad, a well-funded powerful group determined to destroy the United States. Rhodes brutally accused Duncan of associating with Suliman Cindoruk, the bloodthirsty leader of the Sons of Jihad. The accusations focused on a phone call the President made to Cindoruk. Duncan was furious that he had to contend with political insurrection when the future of the United States was in imminent danger.

Chapter Two: Duncan faced his political foes who accused him of being a traitor for his contact with the terrorists. Although Duncan vehemently denied betraying his country, he was not able to share confidential information that could jeopardize the safety of the nation. Because of his inability to be completely transparent, Duncan seemed like he had mixed loyalties, which infuriated his political enemies and made him vulnerable for impeachment. At the end of the chapter, the writer revealed that the interrogation was a practice run for the president which was designed to make him see how bad things could get if he agreed to testify before Congress. The political foes were his own staff, taking positions like those he would expect to face if an interrogation took place. The mock questioning made Duncan acutely aware of his perilous political position.

Chapter Three: The mysterious Russian operative arrived at Regan National, intent on completing her mission. She had a carefully cultivated sexy image designed to distract men and make other women stare in envy. She was dressed in designer clothing and she changed clothing in her chauffeured car, so she would not look recognizable. She carried a matte-black semi-automatic rifle that she named Anna Magdalena.

Chapter Four: Duncan called his faithful assistant, Carolyn, to check on new developments related to Suliman Cindoruk and the threat to the United States. He listed to the news reports about his political peril including his possible impeachment. Duncan remembered life in the White House with his late wife and he missed her.

Chapter Five: Duncan met with Dr. Deborah Lane, a specialist who worked at Georgetown in hemotology. She helped him manage his potentially life-threatening blood disorder. Lane found bruising and evidence that his medical condition was deteriorating. The doctor drew blood and told him that he platelet count was low, and she told the president that he was in danger of internal bleeding and a stroke. He refused treatment that could compromise his ability to think clearly and they compromised on high levels of steroids.

Chapter Six: Suliman Cindoruk arranged for a one-day celebration of his team in his penthouse completed with eight women who received princely sums for entertainment. He congratulated himself on his plans to reboot the world.

Chapter Seven: Lester Rhodes went to visit Duncan in the Oval Office. Duncan and Rhodes met to discuss Rhode's suspicions that Duncan was aligned with terrorists. Duncan became angry and challenged him, giving Rhodes a summary of the magnitude of the threat looming over the country. Rhodes was unmoved, as if nothing that Duncan said mattered. He said he was going to meet with his caucus and move forward with a politically based investigation of President Duncan.

Chapter Eight: Duncan was disappointed that Rhodes was not going to support him through this crisis. He met with Danny Akers, his White House Counsel and shared memories of their lives together. Duncan admitted that he felt that his only option was to deal with the situation on his own, independent of security officers and staff. Duncan admitted that the ideas was full of danger, but he was willing to proceed.

Chapter Nine: Bach waited for her contact in Washington. Intelligent, she looked at the memorials and landmarks in the city and listened to classical music. She met her contact and they exchanged information at a pub using a crossword puzzle. She was optimistic that she would complete her assignment that day unless the weather became rainy.

Chapter Ten: In the Situation Room, Duncan's staff met to discuss the threats to the nation. They talked about problems in the Middle East and the impact on the United States. Duncan called the mother of a nineteen-year-old soldier who was killed on a military mission and later met with staff about a Medicaid issue.

Chapter Eleven: Carolyn and Duncan entered the Situation room, fearing that an attack on the United States was imminent. When they realized that the problem was elsewhere, Duncan was relieved. He had to make a difficult decision to eliminate two high-value targets in the war in the Middle East. Duncan was forced to decide whether to attack a target knowing that one of the targets brought his own children as a shield for the attack. Duncan asked all his advisers for their opinion. The importance of killing the terrorists was clear but they all knew that seven innocent children would die. Duncan listened to their opinions and decided to strike.

Chapter Twelve: Duncan thought about a call he received on his personal cell phone. He waited impatiently for a visitor, a female who was scheduled to meet with him about the threat to the nation. Carolyn was the only person in the nation who knew about the meeting between the woman and Jon.

Chapter Thirteen: A girl entered Duncan's room wearing work boots, torn jeans, and a tee shirt. She was waif thin and the right side of her head was shaved in a buzz cut. Duncan demanded that she say the code words to verify that she was the person he expected to meet. She knew that the code was *Dark Ages*. Her voice was heavily accented, and she had metal in her head from being attacked. She left an envelope. While she was there, the lights in the White House flickered as they had done sporadically over the past weeks.

Chapter Fourteen: Duncan took a picture of his late wife, Rachael, from a drawer. In the picture, she was blotchy and weak from cancer treatments. To anyone else, it would have been Rachael Carson Duncan at her worst but to Jon she looked beautiful, strong and at peace. He met with his staff and told them that he had to go off the record to save the country. He took off all monitoring equipment and entered a tunnel that took him away from the White House and safety.

Chapter Fifteen: Duncan entered the underground parking garage, got into a car, and drove out into the city.

Chapter Sixteen: The writers went into Duncan's college years, when he was a student in Professor Waite's class. Duncan was unable to answer a question accurately and a female student gave a precise, brilliant response. Duncan turned to look at the female and felt like the air was knocked out of him. The woman was Rachael Carson, a student who beat him out of being the editor in chief of the law review. He attempted to impress her, but he was awkward. Duncan wrote an entertaining self-deprecating poem and read it to her and her friends. She was adequately impressed, and their relationship developed.

Chapter Seventeen: Duncan thought about Rachael's valiant battle with cancer and her funeral. He realized that while he was mourning the loss of the love of his life, he also had to face national threats and potential attacks. He went to Mandy's apartment, missing his late wife.

Chapter Eighteen: Mandy, a friend of Rachael and Jon's, used her skill with make up to help Jon change his appearance before he went out to meet the terrorists. He told her that he was going out to meet someone, and Mandy thought that he had a date and did not want to be recognized. He did not correct her.

Chapter Nineteen: Duncan tried to blend in with other people as he made his way to meet with the terrorist. He encountered a homeless veteran of the Gulf War. Duncan stopped to share military experiences with the man and gave him money. Duncan then saw a black man in conflict with police officers. He wanted to help but he had to move to his destination.

Chapter Twenty: Duncan entered a bar where he found his daughter, Lilly. She asked him if he was going to meet with Nina and told him that Nina came to her in Paris and told her that she knew about *Dark Ages*. Duncan told Lilly that he had protection with him because he didn't want to worry her. Knowing that he was in danger, Lilly hugged him and cried.

Chapter Twenty-One: After meeting with Lilly, Duncan took steroids for his blood condition. He hated the pills because her made his thinking clouded. Duncan spoke with Dr. Lane about his medical condition and she urged him to get a treatment to control his platelet count. Duncan proceeded to a ball game where Nina arranged for him to meet Augie and discuss the *Dark Ages*. Although Duncan did not have secret service with him, he was in constant touch by phone with Carolyn.

Chapter Twenty-Two: The assassin known as Bach vomited into a toilet. She wiped the toilet with Clorox wipes to remove any trace DNA. She left the bathroom and joined three men who were selected from a nationwide pool as the deadliest assassins in the world for this mission. The four formed the ground team to eliminate Nina, Augie, and the president.

Chapter Twenty-Three: Augie sat down next to Duncan at the sports stadium. They challenged each other's authority. Augie had a gun but made no attempt to kill Duncan. They discussed the computer virus and the role of the terrorists in trying to destroy the United States. Augie was secretive and revealed far less than Duncan wanted to know.

Chapter Twenty-Four: Duncan focused on Augie, not on his Glock. Duncan knew that Augie and Nina had successfully downed a helicopter in Dubai, hacked into the electrical system at 1600 Pennsylvania Avenue, and created a devastating computer virus. Augie told Duncan that he was aware of the term *Dark Ages,* words that only Duncan's inner circle knew. As soon as Duncan heard that the term had been shared outside that circle, he knew he had a traitor in the White House.

Chapter Twenty-Five: The baseball game ended, and the Nationals left the field. Duncan was in contact with Carolyn to assure his safety. Duncan pressed for information, but Augie was secretive. He was affiliated with the Sons of Jihad, but he no longer wanted to help them advance their brutal mission. He and Nina were willing to share information about the computer virus to stop the *Dark Ages* from happening.

Chapter Twenty-Six: Bach was on a rooftop, poised with the precision of a trained assassin. She saw her target and put her fingers on the trigger.

Chapter Twenty-Seven: Duncan and Augie moved to the exit of the ballfield, intent on leaving without detection. Augie's head dropped down to his phone and tapped his fingers. At that moment, everything went black.

Chapter Twenty-Eight: Katherine Brandt, the vice president, wanted to be the president. She was not pleased that she was second in command to Jon Duncan.

Chapter Twenty-Nine: The lights outside the stadium were out, forcing Duncan and Augie to fee in the dark. Gunfire erupted, killing Nina as she sat waiting outside the stadium in a van.

Chapter Thirty: Duncan, Alex, and the team rushed to safety. Augie was secured in the back of the vehicle, sobbing about Nina's death.

Chapter Thirty-One: Bach left the building after the shooting, remembering Renko, the man who taught her to shoot.

Chapter Thirty-Two: Augie blamed the Americans for Nina's death and refused to cooperate. As the car raced to the White House, another car fishtailed into them and opened fire.

Chapter Thirty-Three: Bach remembered the Serbian soldiers coming to her home when she was a child. She thought about her father's death as she walked into a room where operatives from the assassination outside the stadium were staying. Bach knew that the operatives could no longer function as they needed to complete her mission. She shot the injured operatives in cold blood, so they could not hinder the work they were hired to do.

Chapter Thirty-Four: The president's vehicle was under attack and his team moved into action to keep him safe. The attack on the vehicle continued as they crossed the bridge into Virginia.

Chapter Thirty-Five: Augie was about to go into shock during the attack. Duncan was in touch with Carolyn Brock, Alex, and new FBI Director Elizabeth Greenfield regarding the attack. The terrorists were neutralized but Duncan knew that the attacks were connected to the *Dark Ages* threat.

Chapter Thirty-Six: The Secret Service agents did their job effectively and saved Duncan and his team. They arrived at a secluded location where Carolyn Brock's husband was expecting them.

Chapter Thirty-Seven: Greg Morton, Carolyn's husband, took Duncan and his crew to a safe room. He told Duncan that he saw Carolyn lose a congressional election, miscarry a baby, and help him recover from a heart attack. He said she was never as terrified as she was when she heard about the attack.

Chapter Thirty-Eight: Duncan went into the basement of the structure and contacted his team at the White House using the computer. They discussed the attack, attempting to discern who was responsible and how to prevent future attacks. They discussed the use of the code words, *Dark Ages,* and acknowledged that there was a traitor in the White House inner circle. Because Liz was new, she did not have access to the term when the breach of security occurred. Duncan said that made her the only person in the inner circle he could fully trust.

Chapter Thirty-Nine: Duncan was informed that Nina had died from the attack. Duncan was connected to David, the Director of Mossad. David said that his information indicated that Russia was behind the attack.

Chapter Forty: David said that the intelligence he gathered indicated that the *Dark Ages* threat was going to occur on Saturday so there were just hours to stop the destruction from the computer virus. Duncan continued to try to obtain information from Augie in a desperate attempt to save the nation from destruction. Duncan learned that the Sons of Jihad were focused on destruction through computer access.

Chapter Forty-One: Duncan and his team tried to determine what Suliman wanted to obtain from the computer attack. Suliman did not give them any demand for either action or ransom. They learned that Augie and Nina contacted Duncan, not for ransom as part of a warning.

Chapter Forty-Two: Augie told Duncan that the devasting computer virus was set to go off on Saturday which was the same information that Mossad offered. Duncan collapsed because of the impact of his blood disease and he imagined telling Rachael that he was not ready to die yet.

Chapter Forty-Three: Katherine Brandt heard someone knock on her door at one in the morning. She was given a newspaper with the headlines "The President is Missing." She immediately decided that she needed to speak with Carolyn Brock.

Chapter Forty-Four: Carolyn Brock did not change clothes from the things she wore the day before; it was clear she had been up all night. Katherine spoke with Carolyn online and demanded to know where the president was hiding. Carolyn would not tell her. The two women battled for control knowing that while Katherine would become president, Carolyn was in a position of power.

Chapter Forty-Five: Cindoruk sat on his penthouse terrace, knowing that the destruction of the United States by the devastating computer virus was imminent. He learned that Nina was dead, and he was informed that Augie was being held by Duncan's team.

Chapter Forty-Six: Dr. Lane arrived to provide emergency treatment to Duncan through an IV line. When Duncan recovered, he insisted that one of his agents, a former Navy Seal, would be able to remove the IV line safely.

Chapter Forty-Seven: Duncan and his team met with his staff online to share information about the impending disaster. While he was talking with Carolyn, Liz, and other aids they learned that a computer virus took over pump speeds and valve settings at a building in Los Angeles, clearly indicating that the terrorists were beginning their destruction.

Chapter Forty-Eight: Duncan asked Augie if the events were related to the massive planned computer virus, but Augie had no information.

Chapter Forty-Nine: Duncan traveled on Air Force One to a secluded area for an international summit. He entered a tent where he met with people from a variety of federal agencies who were dedicated to threat mitigation. Based on intelligence information, Duncan learned that the terrorists were not targeting the defense contractor in Los Angeles.

Chapter Fifty: Duncan collaborated with officials from the Center for Disease Control who were worried that the computer virus in California would stop the public water treatment systems. Without clean, potable water, people would not survive. The agency alerted laboratories around the world to be prepared for possible chemical and biological attacks.

Chapter Fifty-One: Noya, head of the Israeli congregation, came with a security detail to the summit. Noya and Duncan were very close, and he trusted the Israeli leader. The German chancellor arrived.

Chapter Fifty-Two: Duncan informed the foreign leaders that the terrorists hacked into the computer software and changed the control settings. The terrorists also disabled the control settings on the equipment to stop any alerts. Duncan learned that the terrorists might have created water shortages for around fourteen million people. The disaster would be far worse than the problems in Flint, Michigan.

Chapter Fifty-Three: Duncan ordered federal agencies to mobilize to protect the people in the nation. He activated the threat response teams and ordered them to prepare for the worst-case scenarios.

Chapter Fifty-Four: Katherine sat in the back of her limo, trying to understand the evolving situation. She imagined what her husband would be like if she became the president. She encountered Lester, who passed by in running gear. They spoke briefly, and Lester offered to throw his support behind her to become president if she agreed to endorse his daughter as a judge.

Chapter Fifty-Five: Lester made his plea to put his daughter on the Supreme Court. Katherine listed to his offer and her mouth dropped open. Lester's daughter was a Harvard grad with impressive credentials and she could receive approval if nominated. Katherine realized that she could make a deal with Lester that would put her in the Oval Office for two and a half terms.

Chapter Fifty-Six: The international leaders ate bagels and fruit before beginning their work. They considered their relationship with Russia.

Chapter Fifty-Seven: Augie admitted that he didn't know much about Nina. She was the computer genius who created the virus, but she never revealed much about her personal life.

Chapter Fifty-Eight: The German Chancellor discussed the 2015 hacking of computers there. The group felt concerned about cyberterrorists, especially those from Russia. Israel was best at cyber defense, but Russia was known to be the best at being on the offense.

Chapter Fifty-Nine: Augie stood before the group of world leaders as they questioned him. Augie had an international team of computer experts available to meet with him to disarm the virus. The computer virus had been dormant for three years and had the capacity to reach every device that receives Internet service from infected providers. Since the Internet connected the world, it had the capacity to impact every technologically advanced nation on earth.

Chapter Sixty: Augie explained that the virus was considered a wiper virus with the capacity to erase all software on a device. The virus would wipe out all health care data, financial records, health records, infrastructure systems, military and security operations, and other systems vital to security and health.

Chapter Sixty-One: Augie stunned the Israeli Prime Minister and the German Chancellor with his assessment of the imminent computer threat. They knew that Russia was behind the threat and Russia's biggest threat was the North Atlantic Treaty Organization (NATO). The other nations knew that NATO had objected to Russia's expansion into other territories. They knew that Russia could hit any other country at any time with the computer virus.

Chapter Sixty-Two: Russian officials arrived in a convoy of black vehicles. Duncan knew that if Russia was behind the computer virus, they would be reluctant to send their president to the summit. The Russian delegation was represented by the prime minister; the president opted not to attend which spoke volumes about the county's involvement in the terrorist threat. The Russia delegation denied responsibility for the computer virus.

Chapter Sixty-Three: Noya Baram and Duncan shared their observations about the threat. Duncan indicated that Russia was concerned that if the computer virus was complete, the United States would counterstrike. Although Russia adamantly denied involvement, the other leaders knew they were responsible.

Chapter Sixty-Four: Bach decided that she was going to end her career as an assassin after this assignment. Pregnant, she wanted to make money from this job and raise her daughter with love, happiness, and every worldly thing she needed. The baby's father was a man she selected deliberately because she felt he was a good genetic candidate. He was a Yale graduate who worked as a radiologist. She slept with him no more than three times a week to protect his potency and left him after she became pregnant. Thinking about her baby, Bach took her gun and slipped into the lake near the secluded site where the multi-national summit was being held.

Chapter Sixty-Five: Duncan spoke with his CIA director and learned that the spread of the computer virus was unlike the tactics usually employed by Russia. Duncan went online and spoke with Carolyn Brock who discussed the vice president's appearance on a national television show. Katherine made it sound like Duncan was missing, creating the potential for a national crisis.

Chapter Sixty-Six: Bach moved through the water and swam toward the summit meeting.

Chapter Sixty-Seven: Bach hid in the woods, thinking about her youth in the Trebevic mountains where Ranko, the redheaded Serbian, taught her to shoot with precision. She remembered the Serbian troops who beat her father to death. Bach then hid in the mountains of Serbia and she remembered the pain she felt. As she moved forward to the summit site, Bach saw a group of coyotes blocking her path. She decided that if she killed the leader, the rest would disperse.

Chapter Sixty-Eight: The Summit leaders discussed invoking NATO sanctions while they received news that the team of computer experts working on the threat had identified the virus.

Chapter Sixty-Nine: Bach walked through the woods to the summit site. She was nearly discovered by Duncan's team and she was forced to hang in a tree to avoid capture.

Chapter Seventy: As the computer team struggled to find the solution to the virus, they discovered that Augie had escaped from an open window.

Chapter Seventy-One: Bach still trapped in a tree, watched two German sentries patrol the area. She knew that if she shot both, their counterparts could know because they would be out of radio contact and the security patrols would come looking for her. She did not want to abort the mission and retreat. As she considered her options, both Germans responded to something they heard on their radios they left the area. Relieved, she moved up the tree to a more secure limb, which afforded her a better position for her assignment.

Chapter Seventy-Two: The security agents scrambled to find Augie while Duncan ordered the computer experts to stay focused on killing the computer virus.

Chapter Seventy-Three: Russian agents shot at a tree where Augie was hiding, splintering a branch. Augie stood by the tree, clutching his chest. Augie said the Russians tried to kill him and Duncan could not tell if the shots were a warning or aimed at Augie. Augie confessed that he was afraid and ran because he did not want to be a captive when the virus finally hit the country.

Chapter Seventy-Four: Perched on a high branch, Bach saw the black tent where the leaders convened for the summit. She saw Duncan and had to decide whether to shoot him.

Chapter Seventy-Five: Augie admitted that he was terrified. He said that Nina feared for her life in Georgia but she wanted to return. She hoped that Duncan would work out an amnesty deal with Georgia to keep her safe. Augie explained that Nina created the brilliant computer virus; his role was to be the hacker who put the virus on servers. Augie said that Nina had been testing Duncan when she came to the White House alone. Augie tested Duncan when he had a gun at the stadium and no secret service stopped him. Augie and Nina thought they could trust Duncan and they planned to stop the virus after they met to discuss amnesty for Nina. Instead, a shooter killed Nina. Duncan asked Augie about the White House traitor.

Chapter Seventy-Six: The Director of the FBI called to tell Duncan that they located Suliman Cindoruk.

Chapter Seventy-Seven: Duncan shared information about the virus with Katherine Brandt and he told her that one of his White House insiders had been a traitor. She denied being the traitor and offered to resign if he did not trust her. Duncan said that the terrorists staged the computer problems in California as a decoy and the actual virus would be far more destructive.

Chapter Seventy-Eight: The computer experts worked frantically to destroy the virus. The virus wiped out each computer used in their work, so they were destroying hundreds of laptops to find a way to stop the virus.

Chapter Seventy-Nine: Duncan refused his vice president's resignation. He told her that he knew about her conversation with Lester Rhodes.

Chapter Eighty: Suliman watched his team recover from their celebratory night of debauchery. He checked his gun and made sure it had a single bullet.

Chapter Eighty-One: The team of agents raced to Suliman's penthouse, intent to capture him.

Chapter Eighty-Two: Suliman's security system alerted him to a breach outside the penthouse. He grabbed his gun and put it under his chin. He was determined to die rather than be captured and tortured.

Chapter Eighty-Three: The agents stormed Suliman's apartment, looking for him.

Chapter Eighty-Four: Suliman escaped and headed for a boat.

Chapter Eighty-Five: The agents told Duncan that Suliman escaped. Duncan was disappointed and fearful that he could not stop *Dark Ages*. He spoke with his old friend, Danny, who reminded him that he was a natural leader and assured him that he would find a way to solve the problem.

Chapter Eighty-Six: Carolyn called Duncan and had Liz on the phone. They discussed giving Katherine a lie-detector test.

Chapter Eighty-Seven: Duncan called the Chief Justice of the Supreme Court and told him to make sure that all of the court members were secure. He also called Lester Rhodes to tell him to keep Congress secure, but Lester thought that Duncan was bluffing to cover the impending hearings.

Chapter Eighty-Eight: Lester ordered his team of six to stay together in the operations room and prepare to speak to him.

Chapter Eighty-Nine: Duncan met with his computer experts and learned that Suliman named the virus Suleman.exe. The virus deleted all files in infected computers. It had a wiper feature, which would overwrite data, making it impossible to retrieve. Duncan frantically encouraged the group to be creative.

Chapter Ninety: Duncan met with his inner circle and told them that one was a traitor. He said if the person came forward and resigned, he would allow them to leave the country. If no one came forward, he would prosecute him or her, for treason.

Chapter Ninety-One: Work continued dismantling the computer virus. Duncan provided suggestions on things to try.

Chapter Ninety-Two: As the group tried new things, Duncan received a call from the FBI.

Chapter Ninety-Three: The FBI Director reported that they were trying to unlock a second phone that Nina left in the van.

Chapter Ninety-Four: Bach continued to sit in a tree, watching the tent. She missed her chance to shoot Augie. Bach thought about the classical music she loved and remembered her mother playing the violin. Her brother also played the violin and he became a talented musician. She thought that it was ironic that she used a rifle and he used a violin.

Chapter Ninety-Five: The members of the summit disbanded to return home to their counties. The Russian, German, and Israeli leaders left before the computer virus was scheduled to hit each saying that they were sorry that they had not resolved the imminent crisis.

Chapter Ninety-Six: Bach watched the leaders depart and she looked for Augie. He did not leave with the group, so she decided that the assassins had to enter the cabin where he was staying.

Chapter Ninety-Seven: The FBI downloaded the contents of Nina's second phone. Nina had been text messaging with the traitor who was sending messages from the White House. The traitor had been communicating with Nina during a meeting with Duncan. The traitor had advance knowledge about activities but did not reveal them to the president. Later, the traitor expressed remorse for not turning the information into authorities.

Chapter Ninety-Eight: Terrorist attackers arrived at the scene of the summit and opened fire on the Secret Service.

Chapter Ninety-Nine: Duncan read texts between Nina and the traitor as gunfire erupted.

Chapter One Hundred: The battle between the agents and the gunfire continued.

Chapter One Hundred One: The virus began to activate computers and devices everywhere.

Chapter One Hundred Two: Suliman got off a private plan and saw the words Virus Activated.

Chapter One Hundred Three: As the computer experts began to panic, the virus stopped.

Chapter One Hundred Four: Bach prepared to leave on a helicopter sent to retrieve her. She heard an explosion and hid in a laundry room.

Chapter One Hundred Five: The computer experts determined that Nina installed a circuit breaker that would stop the virus if a password were entered. The group tried to determine what the password was.

Chapter One Hundred Six: The group tried a number of passwords, but they did not work.

Chapter One Hundred Seven: Duncan ordered the agents to capture Bach alive.

Chapter One Hundred Eight: Bach closed her eyes and thought about her unborn child, Delilah. The door burst open and solders came in to get her. As she thought about her baby, she was content as the Marines rushed her out of the room.

Chapter One Hundred Nine: Casey and Devin, the computer experts, desperately tried to come up with the password to stop the computer virus as the clock to *Dark Ages* raced ahead.

Chapter One Hundred Ten: Duncan called Carolyn and told her that there was less than six minutes until the computer virus went off. He told her that he ordered a search of the vice president's office.

Chapter One Hundred Eleven: The team was aware that time was running out and they tried several random guesses for the password. The FBI director suggested trying Nina's hometown, Sokhumi. It did not work. They tried other words, and none worked. Carolyn said that she was on an intelligence committee and she saw Sokhumi spelled with two u's and no o. It worked perfectly, and the threat was abated.

Chapter One Hundred Twelve: The experts successfully stopped the computer virus. Duncan was then able to focus on identifying the traitor in his midst. The traitor planted a phone in the vice president's office to tie her to the crime.

Chapter One Hundred Thirteen: Suliman stared at his phone and saw the words Virus Disabled. He knew that Nina had sabotaged his plan.

Chapter One Hundred Fourteen: Duncan met with Carolyn and then spent time with his daughter, Lilly.

Chapter One Hundred Fifteen: Duncan talked with Danny and with others they listened to the cable news stories about the computer virus threat.

Chapter One Hundred Sixteen: Carolyn read the texts between Nina and the traitor. Nina obtained information about the location of Duncan's daughter from the traitor and approached her with the phrase *Dark Ages* to get her father's attention. Duncan asked all of them to help think of a potential password to stop the virus. Ultimately, Carolyn had the correct answer.

Chapter One Hundred Seventeen: Duncan spoke to his inner circle and told them that the conference with them was a ruse. He said they already figured out the password, but he thought only the traitor would know the word. When Carolyn knew the word, he found his traitor.

Chapter One Hundred Eighteen: Carolyn attempted to downplay her role in the situation and Duncan asked to have the chance for them to speak without anyone else in the room.

Chapter One Hundred Nineteen: Duncan confronted Carolyn about her betrayal. She was angry, and she said that if she had been a man, she would have been president. Duncan never saw this side of her before and he was shocked at the person he once trusted.

Chapter One Hundred Twenty: Suliman stared at the headlines and knew that Nina added a password to the computer virus. He heard men chasing him and he vowed not to escape. He knew he did not have the courage to kill himself with his own gun. He put his hands together to make it appear that he was holding a weapon and aimed at the men who fatally shot him.

Chapter One Hundred Twenty-One: Katherine offered to resign again. Duncan knew that she plotted with the Speaker of the House against him, but he refused to accept her resignation.

Chapter One Hundred Twenty-Two: Jail guards questioned Bach. She asked to be allowed to bear her daughter in America. Bach wanted her brother to adopt her daughter and in exchange, Bach would tell everything she knew about her crimes.

Chapter One Hundred Twenty-Three: Duncan strolled through the rose garden with Augie and thanked him for assistance. Duncan offered to help him get immigration papers and a job.

Chapter One Hundred Twenty-Four: Duncan called the King of Saudi Arabia and discussed Saudi royal family members financially supporting the Sons of Jihad. They also paid Bach to act as an assassin. The Saudis captured her.

Chapter One Hundred Twenty-Five: Duncan met with the Russian ambassador and accused Russia of involvement in the computer virus. He said that Bach didn't attack until Russia left the summit.

Chapter One Hundred Twenty-Six: Lester Rhodes canceled the select committee meeting and invited Duncan to speak before Congress.

Chapter One Hundred Twenty-Seven: The Speaker of the House announced Duncan and he took a moment to savor the good feelings associated with surviving the threat to the nation.

Chapter One Hundred Twenty-Eight: Duncan gave a speech to Congress and the American people describing the computer virus threat. He named the heroes and identified Suliman Cindoruk and Russia as the villains.

Epilogue: Duncan's approval ratings rose after his speech and the Speaker was angry with him. Carolyn Brock was hit with a twenty-count indictment accusing her of treason and other charges. Duncan received the medical treatment he needed to restore his health. His daughter returned to her normal life, Duncan sent someone to help the homeless veteran he met and worked to help unarmed citizens were attacked by police.

MOTIFS

There were multiple motifs present in the book. The code name, *Dark Ages,* was a powerful motif indicating that without computer access, the nation would lose all technological access and would plunge into the Dark Ages. Since all utilities including the production of electricity, water, and waste disposal were tied into technology, the attack would quickly have the infrastructure resources present during the actual Dark Ages. The nation would lose public water and people would be forced to consume water of uncertain supply and questionable quality. Diseases eradicated in the modern world would return and people would surely die. Every part of the country would be dark without electric power. Manufacturing and production would be impossible. The monetary system would collapse without technology and people would have no resources for trade. The entire health care system would fail; it would be impossible to operate hospitals, clinics, or medical practices without electricity, computer access to records, and water for sanitation. In every way, the term Dark Ages was appropriate because it would bring physical darkness after sunset while it would have taken the nation to a bleak time in history before modern civilization.

Another motif in the book was the battles Jon Duncan fought both internally and externally. Because of his blood disorder, he was in constant danger of experiencing a stroke or hemorrhage. Either event could have left him dead or incapacitated. While he feared leaving his daughter an orphan, Duncan also knew that he had to do what was best for the country. His external battles were less clear. He had the impending threat of being impeached, an assassin targeting him, a close staff member who betrayed him, and the imminent collapse of the entire national technology system. The balance between his internal and external threats were ongoing points of suspense throughout the entire book.

Additionally, Bach's name and love of music were powerful motifs for this complicated character. She loved beauty and embraced the concept of a family, as evidenced by her love for her unborn daughter and her passion for classical music. Because of life circumstances, her days were fully of ugliness. She saw and experienced unspeakable brutality in her homeland. Circumstances forced her to become an assassin. The motif of her name and love for beautiful purity were reminders that no one is ever just good or evil and life circumstances impact us all.

THEME

The theme of this book was a classic tale of good versus evil. Jon Duncan was the classic protagonist. He was raised by a single mother after his father died in an accident. Duncan had no financial resources to help him succeed; he became a military hero in the elite Army Rangers before he went onto stellar sports and political careers. The clear antagonist throughout the book was Suliman Cindoruk, the blood thirsty leader of the Sons of Jihad. This evil terrorist was willing to cause death and destruction throughout the United States by destroying every computer in the country and eliminating access through a deadly computer virus. The theme also focused on the ways that life circumstances impact people and cause them to adopt behaviors that may be outside their moral compass. For example, Bach loved family and art, but she became a brutal killer without remorse or empathy. Nina and Augie were impacted by their circumstances and even Carolyn's behavior was impacted by her resentment about being removed from contention as a presidential hopeful.

ACRONYM GUIDE

FBI referred to the Federal Bureau of Investigations.
CIA referred to the Central Intelligence Agency.
NATO referred to the North Atlantic Treaty Organization.

DISCUSSION QUESTIONS

1. Do you think that Bill Clinton, as one of the writers, relied on his own experiences as president for any of the book?
2. In your opinion, do you think the United States is adequately prepared for a cyberattack?
3. Which nations would support the United States today if we were threatened by an attack? Which countries would support the terrorists?

THOUGHT PROVOKING QUESTIONS

1. Duncan was willing to go rogue to meet with the terrorists. This was exceedingly dangerous. Do you think he was wrong to risk his life when his daughter just lost her mother?

2. Do you believe that Duncan was grieving so much for Rachael that he was more willing to die than he might have been if Rachael had not succumbed to cancer?

3. Lester made a brazen offer to Katherine which would have benefited each of them. Do you think actual politicians behave that way? If yes, what can be done to change things for the better?

4. Do you think that Duncan and Katherine will ever develop mutual trust and respect? How essential do you think it is for a president and vice president to have a trusting and respectful relationship?

5. If the computer virus occurred, how prepared would the United States be for survival without technology? Do you think the nation depends too much on technology?

6. Do you believe that the United States is vulnerable to a computer virus attack today? Which nations are our greatest threat? What can people do to protect themselves?

7. Do you believe that Bach's brother will adopt her child? What challenges will the child face? Would it be better if an unknown family adopted the child? Should the father be contacted and given the option to raise his daughter?

8. Duncan was gentle when he thought about his late wife. Do you think his behavior would have been different if she was alive?

9. Why did the Russian president avoid the summit? Do you think that the tension between the United States and Russia today is as problematic as it was when Clinton was president? Should we worry that Russia would attack our technology?

10. Do you think that a cyberattack is less likely than a nuclear attack? Why do you believe that?

11. Who do you think should protect our national security from cyber terrorism? Is it time for an agency to be created to monitor and deal with this threat? Why don't we have an agency devoted to this yet?

12. Nina and Augie were very young. What kinds of life events caused them to work to develop such a dangerous cyber threat? Are there other young people who vulnerable to doing the same thing?

13. Nina was a genius in programming. Augie was a brilliant hacker. Do you believe that they used their talents appropriately?

14. Lester was an unscrupulous person who wanted to benefit himself and his family. He was not punished for his actions. What do you think would have been an appropriate way to punish him? Should the press be informed of his offer to Katherine? What would that do to his career? What would it do to Katherine's career?

15. Do you think Lilly was in danger? Nina went to find Lilly in Paris and had access to speak to her. Are presidential family members in danger from terrorists? If yes, what can be done to protect them?

CONCLUSION

Thank you for reading this book!

If you enjoyed the book, we would appreciate it if you could post a review of it on Amazon!

As a way of thanking you for purchasing *this* book, we would like to give you another book as a gift: *Stoicism: The Art of Living a Modern Stoic and Happy Life Now*.

If you would like a copy, please visit:
http://NoscoPublishing.com/offer/
Regards,
Nosco Publishing

Made in the USA
Lexington, KY
29 August 2018